I0647271

Seventy-Five

Connectivity through the Ages
by Terry Wild and Lori Joseph

J²B Publishing

Cover and Book Design by Rich Mills
www.streamrunstudios.com

Editing by Julie Haase
www.Copysitter.com

J2B Publishing, LLC
4251 Columbia Park Road
Pomfret, MD 20675
www.j2bllc.com

Library of Congress Control Number: 2022922851

Seventy-Five

ISBN: 978-1-954682-37-5

My friend Terry Wild turned seventy-five on January 18, 2022. A simple exchange to wish him a happy birthday led to this creative endeavor.

The concept of *Seventy-Five* is a testimonial to *real* life, not the embellished life people gravitate to on social media. Our society has experienced a deep decline in empathy over the last three decades. We hope Terry's images with my words will provoke and stimulate you to look at the ordinary and to feel something. If *Seventy-Five* causes you to pause, reflect, or laugh, then we will have succeeded. If you are inspired to look more closely at your daily life and your impact on our natural world and mindfully do something kind for another person, it's a huge win.

Terry captured photos daily, and it was important to him to show the randomness of daily life and how we take the ordinary for granted. I received the images and often sat with them before writing, allowing time to consider the many aspects of how a picture can tell a story or a thought. Because we live in a time of accelerated information, I kept the verse concise. The arc or the journey of *Seventy-Five* is left to the individual reader as each photo/poem stands alone.

Surrounded by life's intricate beauty and abundance, I am honored to have created *Seventy-Five* with Terry.

Lori Joseph

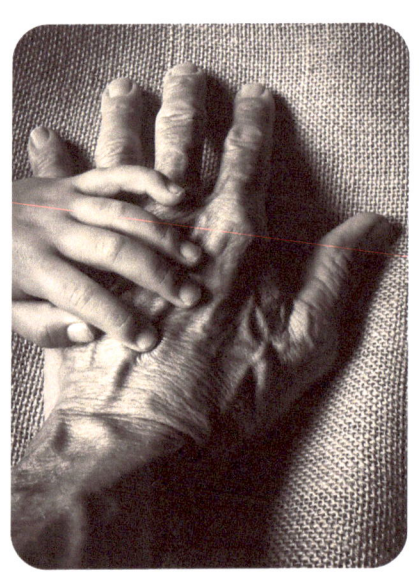

Well, becoming seventy-five years old was, for some reason, a revelation. It crept up on me. It was challenging to my post-polio syndrome mobility and creative intuition. The desire to be "out and about" was diminishing. "In and around" was manageable. Seventy-five—I have reached a time of transition between birth and death.

Then, unexpectedly, Lori Joseph called me to wish me a happy birthday. Lori is a work associate, friend, and writer/poet. She suggested we generate a project together—a picture a day up to seventy-five for which she would create a poetic union. Despite physical limitations, the idea ignited acceptance in me.

As long as I can remember, the visual world has been my teacher. People, places, and things have become my life observations. Technology has developed to the point at which my iPhone is a simple tool to qualitatively harvest all that reveals itself. At seventy-five years of age, the tendency is to deal with each day as different and potentially your last. As a result, the commonplace can become complex and symbolic. Pictures can become much more than what they appear to be.

Accompanied with metaphorical expressions, the combination can transport the viewer to a higher level of understanding.

With our exchange, Lori has somehow been able to compose words that bring associative insight to each image. Her unique perceptions helped me find deeper meaning with each image. She confirmed and renewed my belief that images can help us have reflections about a more attentive world.

Lori's inspired perceptions have brought this project to wonderful heights.

Terry Wild

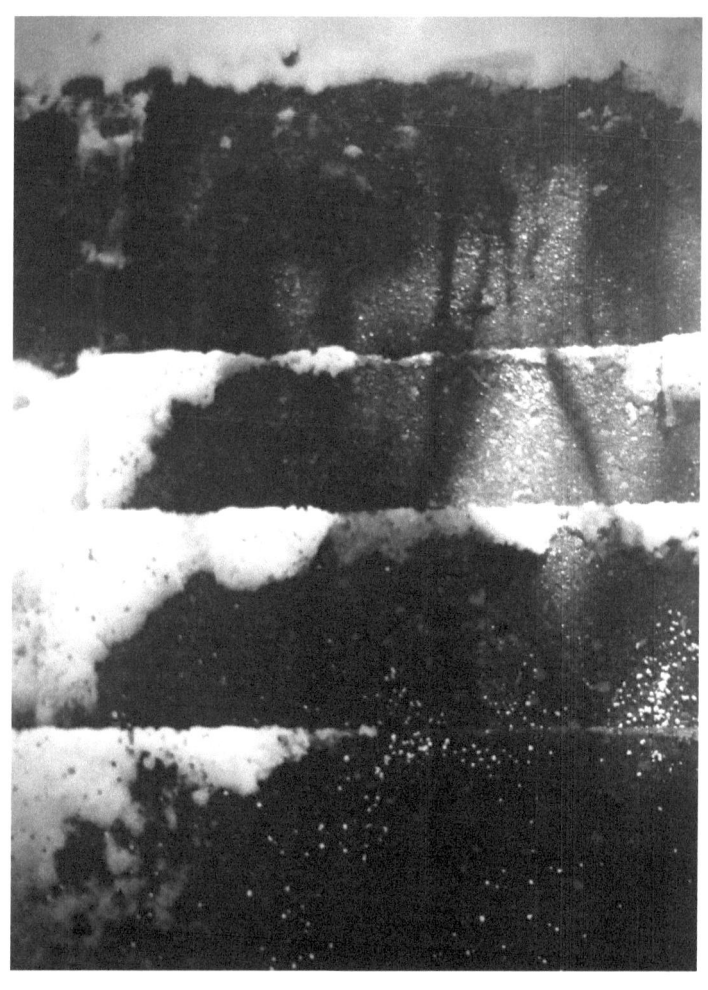

Fulfilling a dream
is showing up and taking the first step.

So much of one's life appears a bit fuzzy
until perspective unfurls divine beauty.

Communal Empathy

Abandon self-absorption, prejudice, and violence.
Feel the flesh, the cellular structure, and all of life's segments
wanting to keep us together.

Peeling back those crepey layers
exposes one's true essence.

Trying to make sense and create order
man creates structure under the heavens.
Given time and wisdom, he realizes
his beliefs have fenced him in.

The Nursing Home

What you see is a stark contrast
to the vibrant souls contained.
Imagine the centuries of lifetimes,
paths taken, and words spoken.

Stamens and Pistils
Guys and Gals
Confusion and Pell-Mell

Wrinkles are a natural consequence,
to map your trips around the sun.

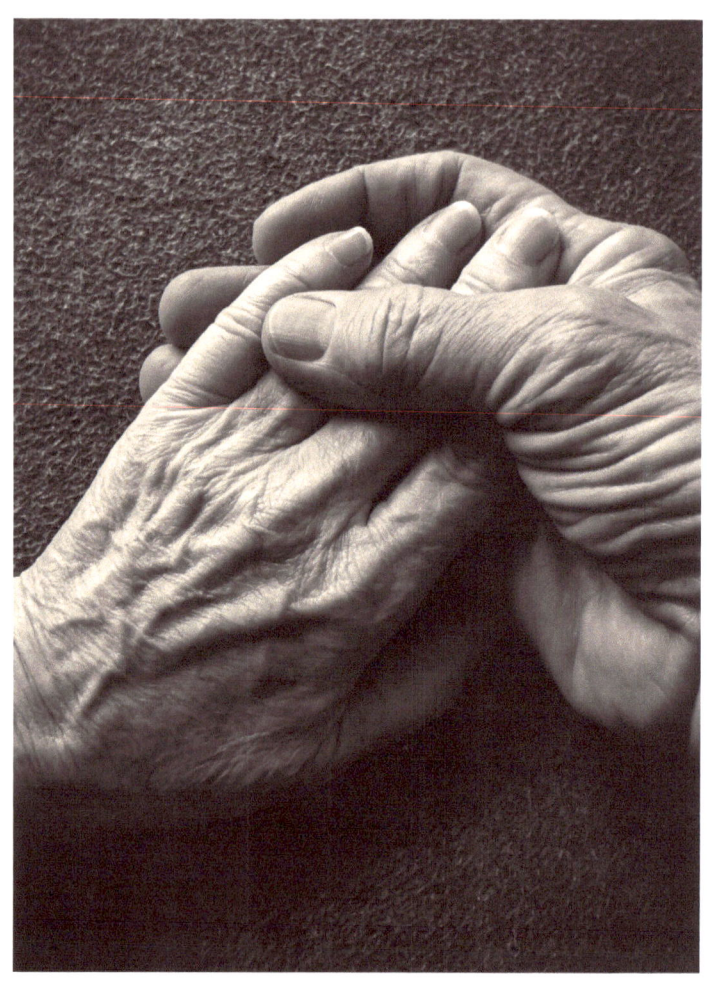

Holding Hands

Timeless is our innate desire
for tenderness and nourishment.

Do I know you? You look familiar.
I'm trying to place where we've met before.
Was it the university or the stable?
Did you prepare my taxes?
Suture my broken heart?
I'm sure it'll come to me.
I feel so much better now, seeing you.
That's all that really matters.

Some cabbage heads are denser than others.
But when you listen to one leaf at a time,
tremendous stories unfold.

Pepper Joy

It's remarkable to have both the sunrise and sunset
evident in the flesh of a pepper.
It brings joy to know it comes from the ancient earth,
complete with seeds for the future.

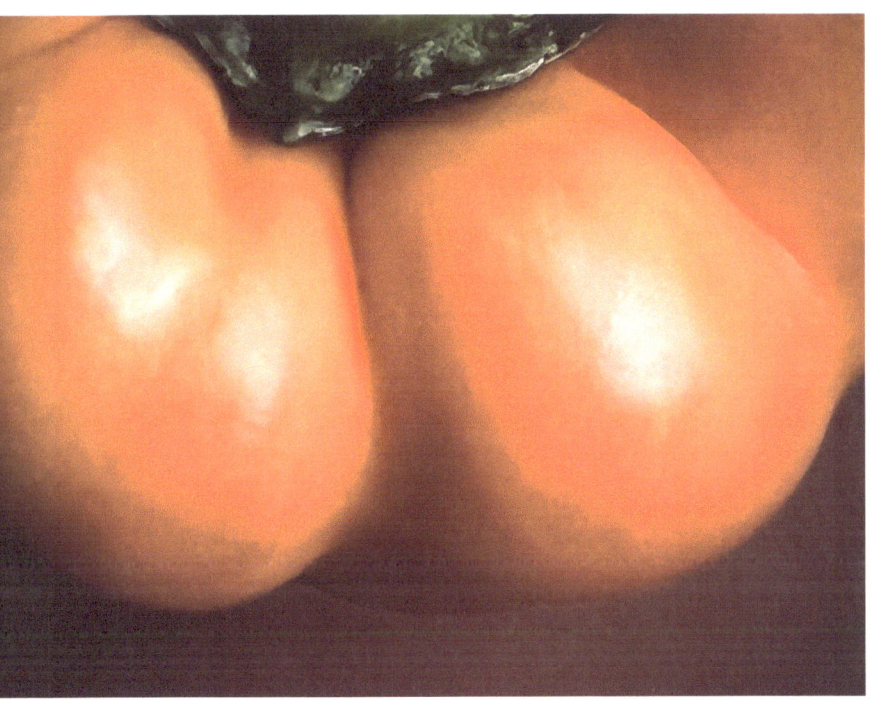

Tapioca Pot

For mind-altering bubbles,
just add water!

Empty nest . . . or is the nest empty?
Interpretation subject to change.

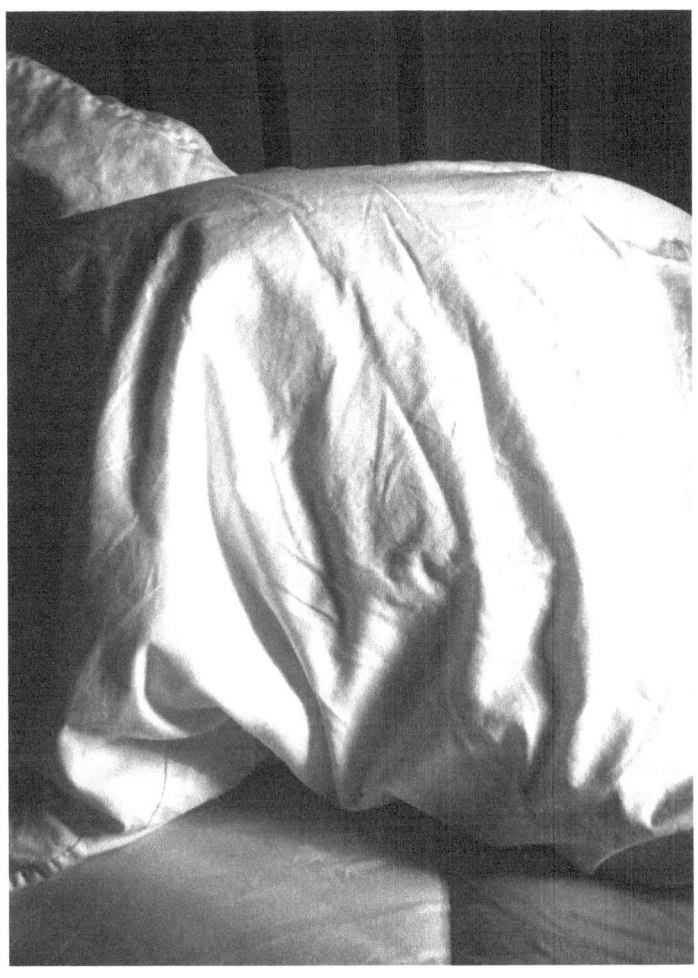

Church Dinner

Symbolic of a congregation
Some may be slightly askew
but stacked up
there is a foundation
of fellowship.

Savory Offering

I see a forest.
A savory offering takes me from this moment
to a garden from the past
where I stood barefoot on the damp earth,
saturated with the scent of fresh herbs.

How lucky am I to know the subtle shifts
of the garden's fragrance as the day stretches on.

And now, before me as I'm about to partake,
I give thanks for my roots.

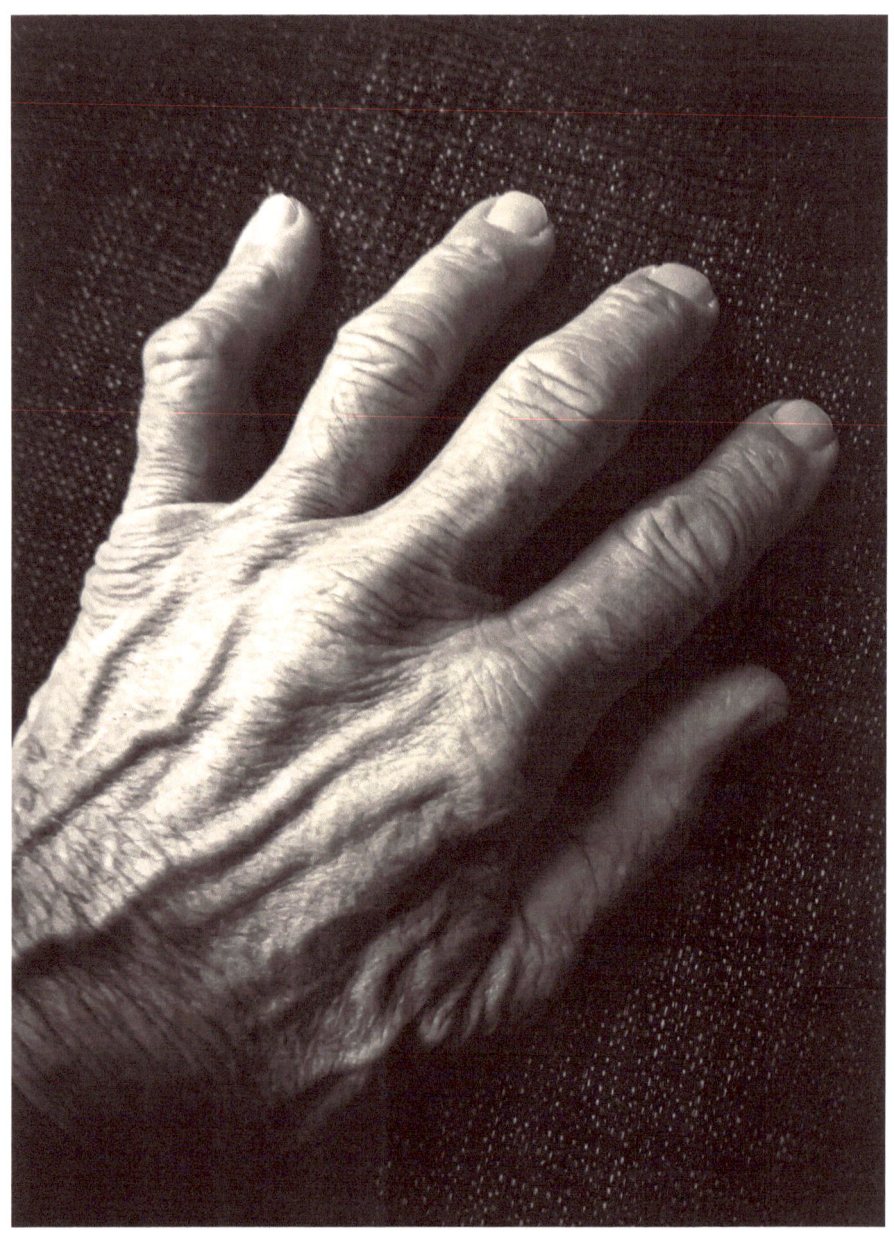

This Hand

This hand
opens a door
holds a baby
works the earth

This hand
stacks firewood
carries love
holds broken hearts

This hand
frames my vision
clutches a camera
holds a trumpet

This hand
prepares food
plants seeds
leads the way

This hand
all my life
has washed
my right

Love and candy are hard to resist.

Dear Watson, do you ever wonder who was the first person to stick their tongue out at another?

Texture, grain, beauty.
It's all about making the cut.

Thought to have originated in ancient Egypt.
Our daily bread, infused with rosemary for
remembrance of sour leavening's lasting presence.

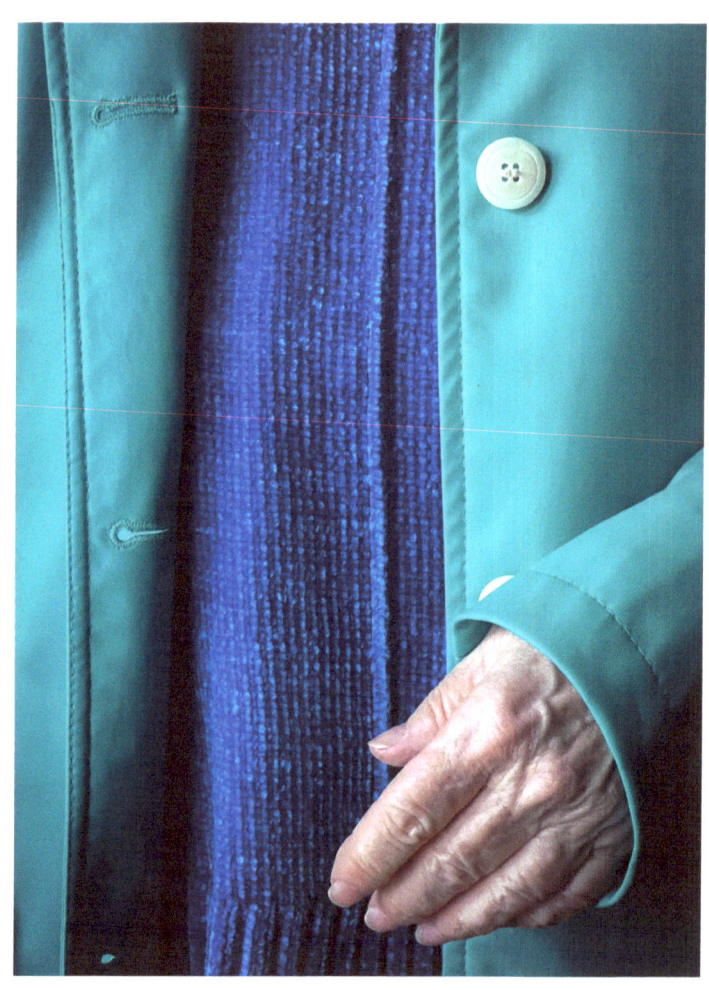

Calm and balanced
clothed in hues
to make it so.

We give pills a lot of credit.
Plain looking, we expect them to know
exactly where to go to help our body.
We might know their origin,
intended purpose, date of expiration
but do they play well with others?

One cannot dream among the trees
with so many red lights, warnings, and rules.

A Road, a Steamroller, a Man with a Bucket of Paint
Converge to make sense, to keep order
Temporary at best.
With each day, there is a constant
Pressure and battle with the elements.
Even healing rains begin to seep and erode
Leaving bits of sun for tomorrow.

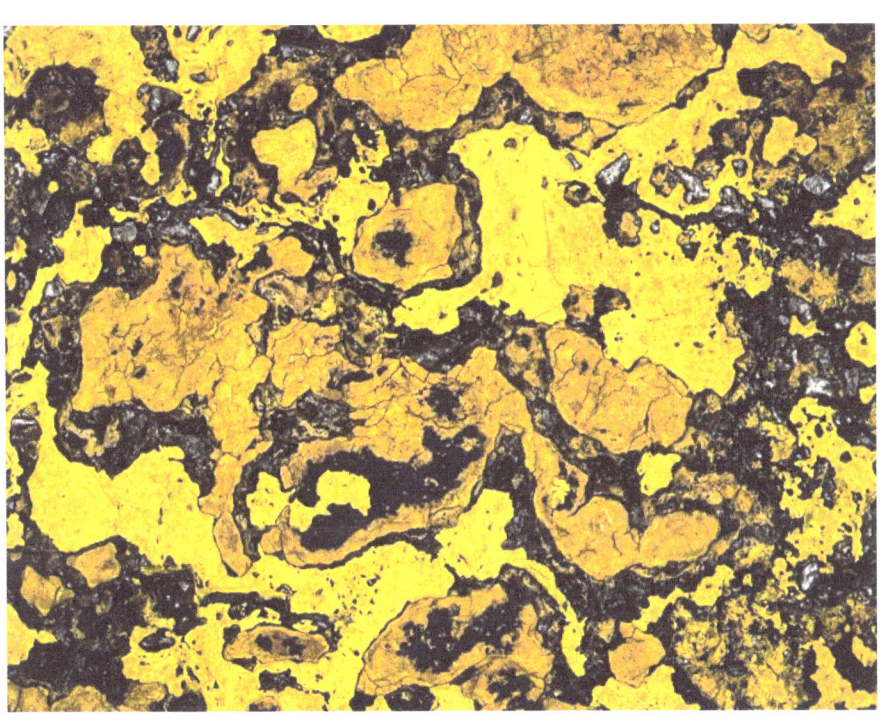

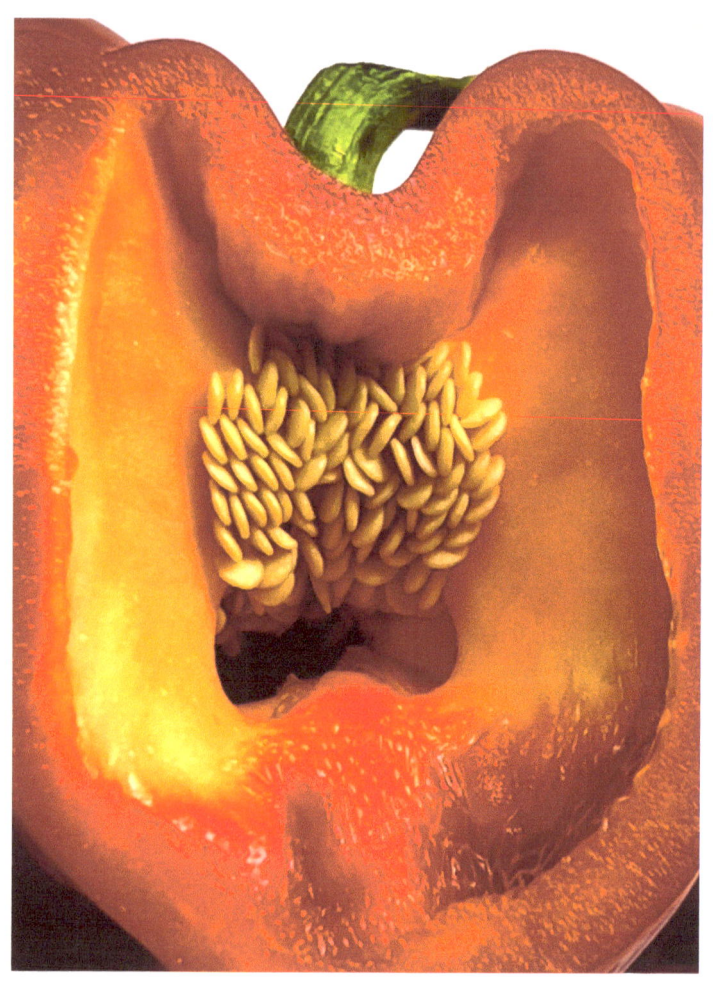

It's only a matter of time
before one gives voice to the seeds planted.

Human vs. Romaine

We both have thick ribs in our mid-section to hold us upright.
Both contain a high percentage of water and benefit from sunlight.
Romaine provides vitamins and nutrients to humans.
Humans plant and provide nutrients to the soil.

It's more of a give and take.

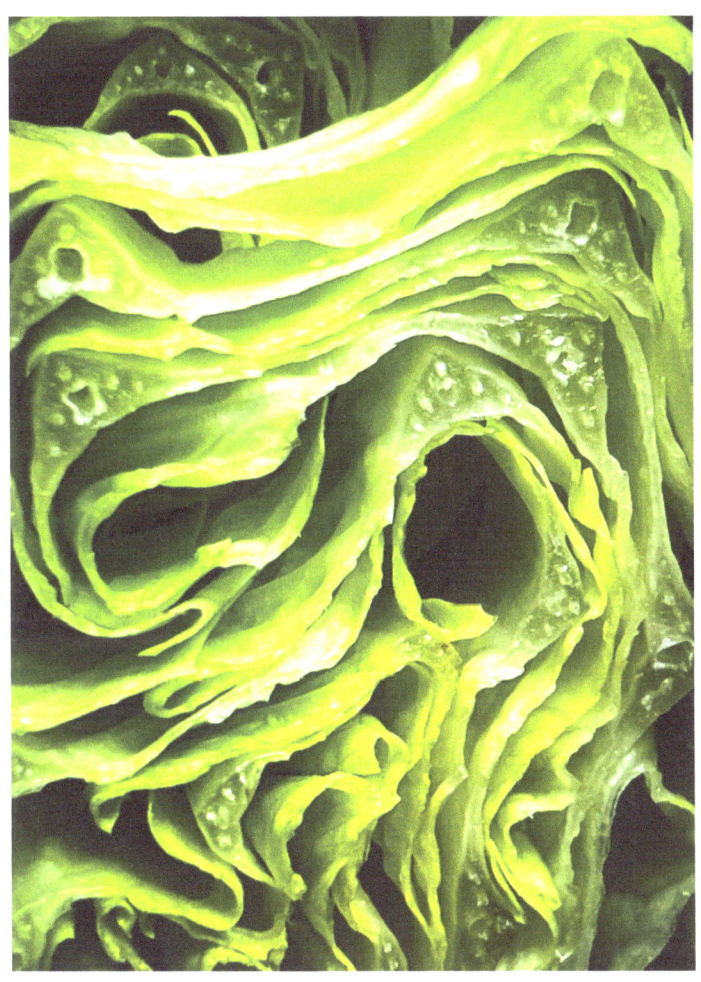

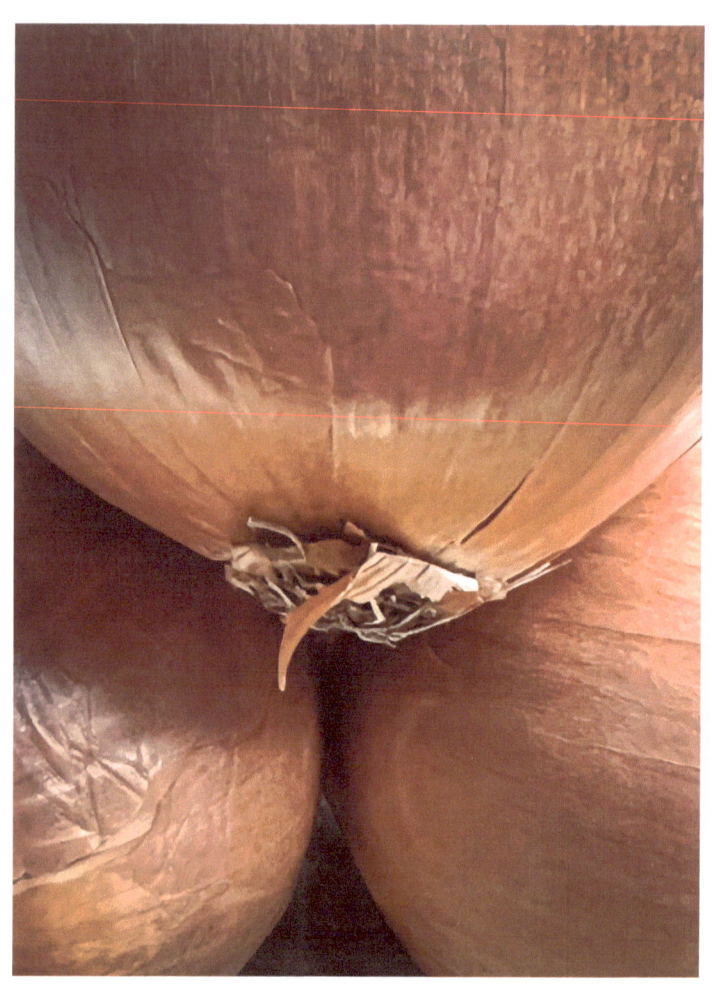

Independence begins
when the umbilical cord
is gone.

Community Wellness

Introducing Baby Spinach,
Heirloom Tomato, the Onion,
English Cucumber,
Slim Radish and the Pine Nut Family
ready to perform.

Optimism

All by itself, this little washer believes it can
distribute the weight of the world.

A long line of empty handicap spaces
can be both good and bad news.
We're either prepared for the worst
or medicine is doing its job.

Beautiful Imperfection

Sometimes when I look up into the trees
I see our world
There are limbs reaching for light
There are limbs broken and crooked

There are scars on bark
Even some man-made

Some trees grow tall, create a canopy
Some lean in one direction more than others

Some retain their shape and color
While others shed and regrow

There are fragrant trees and notable trees
prickly and historic trees
There are trees with sticky resin or sap
the kind you likc to tap

Sometimes when I look up into the trees
I see our world
Alive and well.

Blind Sunset

This blind reminds me of the heart's ability
to open and shut.
With a gentle twist we leverage light to suit.

Turning six, we celebrate the known.
At seventy-six, we celebrate the unknown.

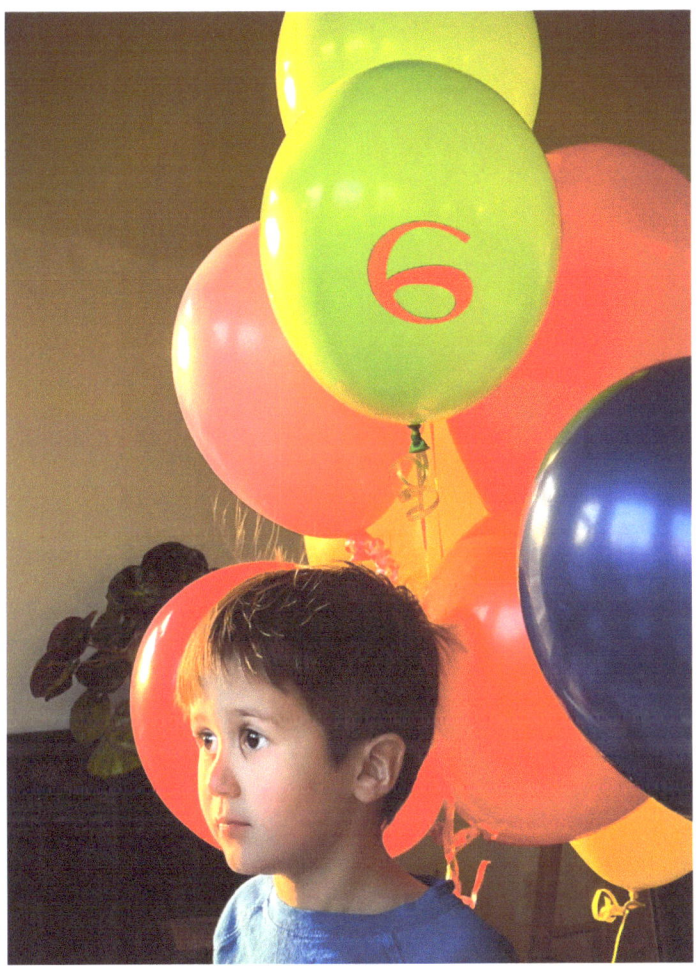

Through body, mind, and spirit,
you have the power of connectivity.

It's Race Day
Behind the screen
The competition is fierce
Raindrops pick up their pace
Sliding across the sill in record time

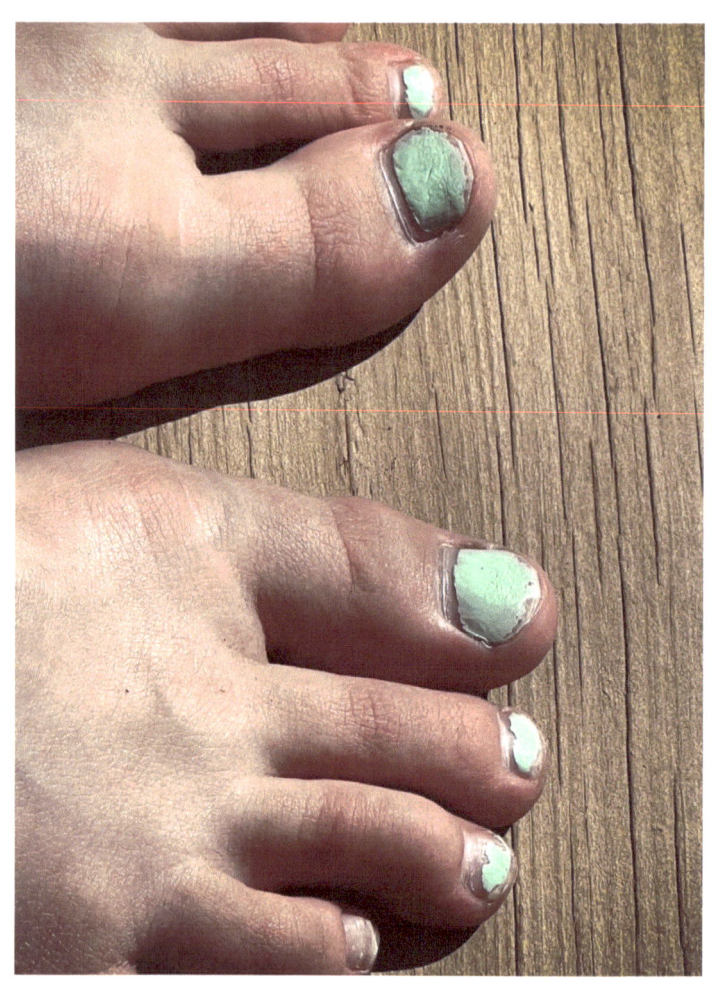

Minted

Penny minted her toes.
Their value holds
Even when the shine wears off.

Tetrachromatic Vision

With such a rich spectrum of color,
I wonder if chickens experience egg envy?

He turned away
for the last time.
Setting boundaries,
never again
to pass through
the whitewash.

These Chops

Behind a flesh veil I smile
These chops serve me well
They form speech
Grind and clench
They give shape
Take nourishment
They're sensitive too

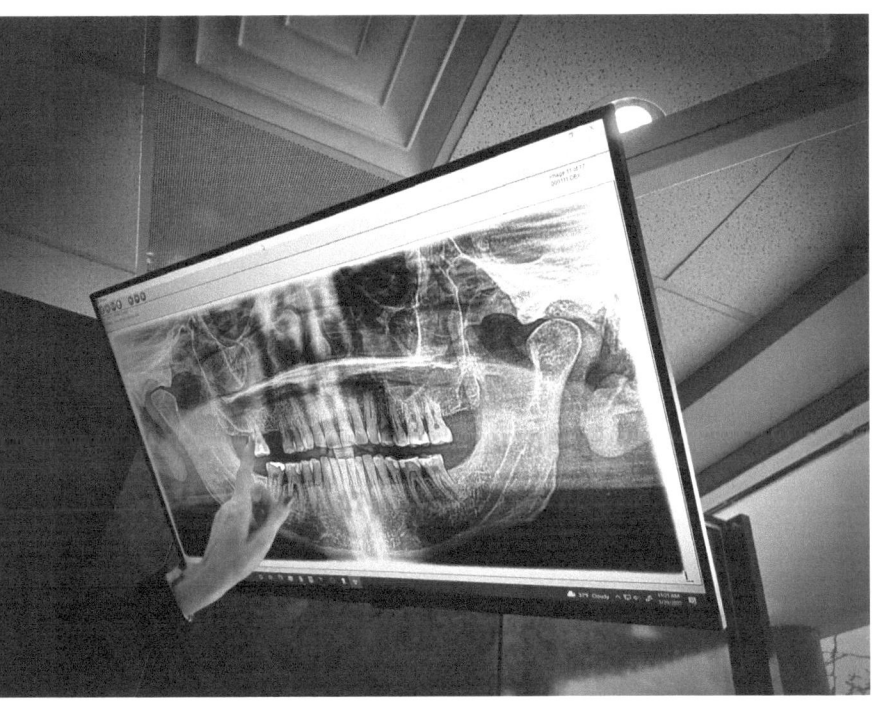

Acropolis Clematis

Motivational magenta flowers
with a pom-pom to cheer you on
inspire optimism
lift you
without saying a word.

Sometimes when we're feeling blue
we have to rely on our inner beauty
and that's okay.

Fibrous texture
Myriad of color
You give me such joy
I dream
of a good yarn.

Every spring I wish I could be a daffodil
with rapid growth, natural defense
with eagerness to bloom.

But then I consider not all humans are as toxic
as the daffodil and manage to thrive year-round.

The little tree-shaped vegetables
remind me of deforestation.

With every bite of broccoli,
I wish for better.

Lift me up
I want to stretch and reach
Touch your lingering softness
Before I drift away.

Snow Shovel

It all starts with a plan
Clear the steps and then the walkway

Scoop and throw
Scoop and throw
Look up, look out
Scoop and throw

The rhythm
The weight
Your posture
Your dreams

Scoop and throw
Scoop and throw
Look up, look back
Scoop and throw

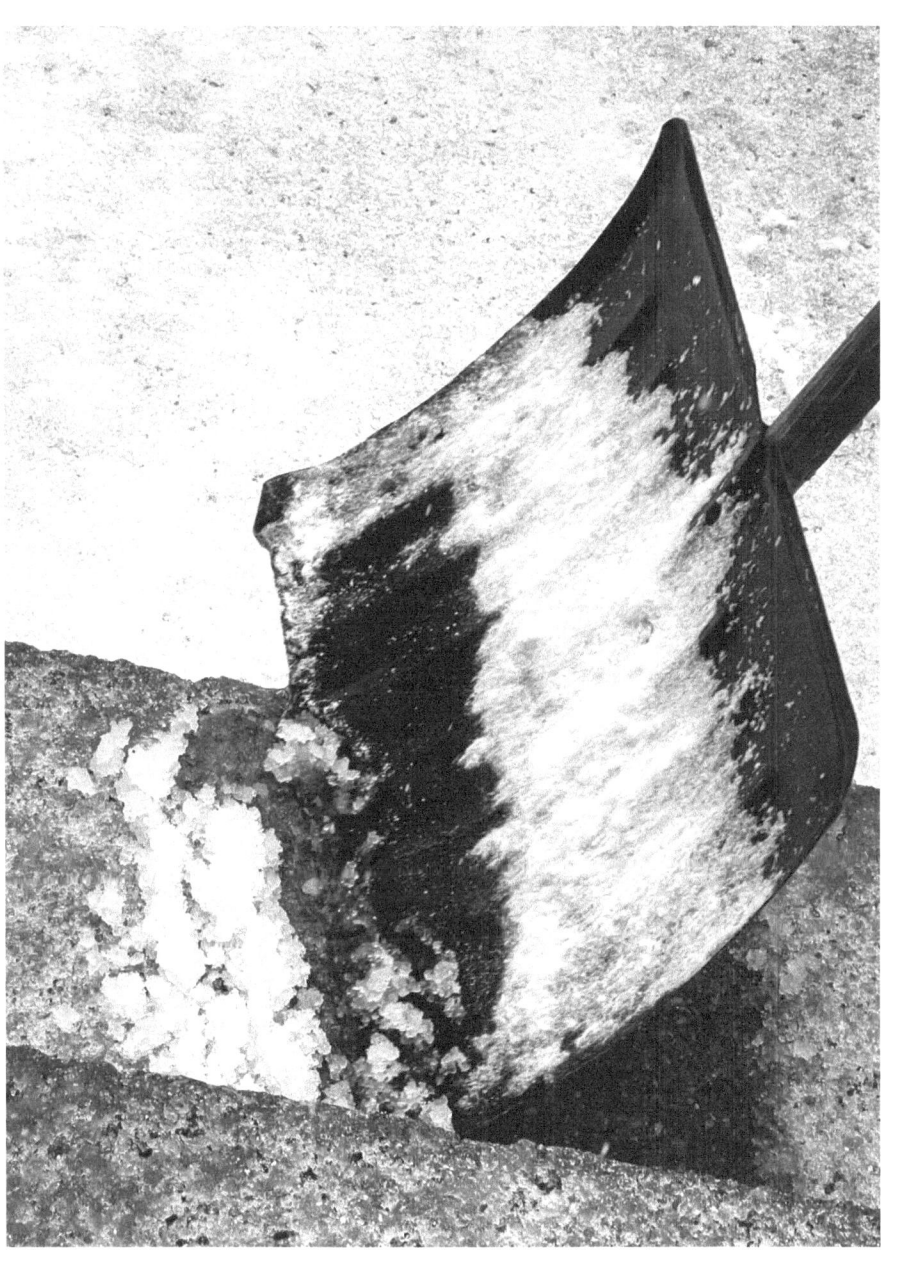

Blue Sky Contradiction

Whether you enter a school, a church,
or your home
what is said for society
when surveillance has become
an acceptable constant?

However fragmented our personal views,
it is essential to understand
we are one.

Before the wolf desired sheep's clothing
shearing was not necessary.

Scrubbing the stovetop
reminds me
of conversations and movements
aimed to dissolve prejudice.

An offered son collects
the offering,
for the Offered Son.

Harmonious Life

The very first note of a song you heard
remains within you.

Predestined to strike a chord
the Universe resonates with twelve notes.

Care to play along?

They call me Frankie
after Ol' Blue Eyes.
It must be my swagger!

Two by Two

Roll in.
Roll out.
This American dream,
duplicated
over and over.
Dare you dream
of less?

Unnoticed

The line painters in the world attempting
to keep us safe.

Infrastructure Painted with Caution

Life is chipping away.
Pacemakers and pipes.
Hip joints and trestles.
Nothing lasts forever.

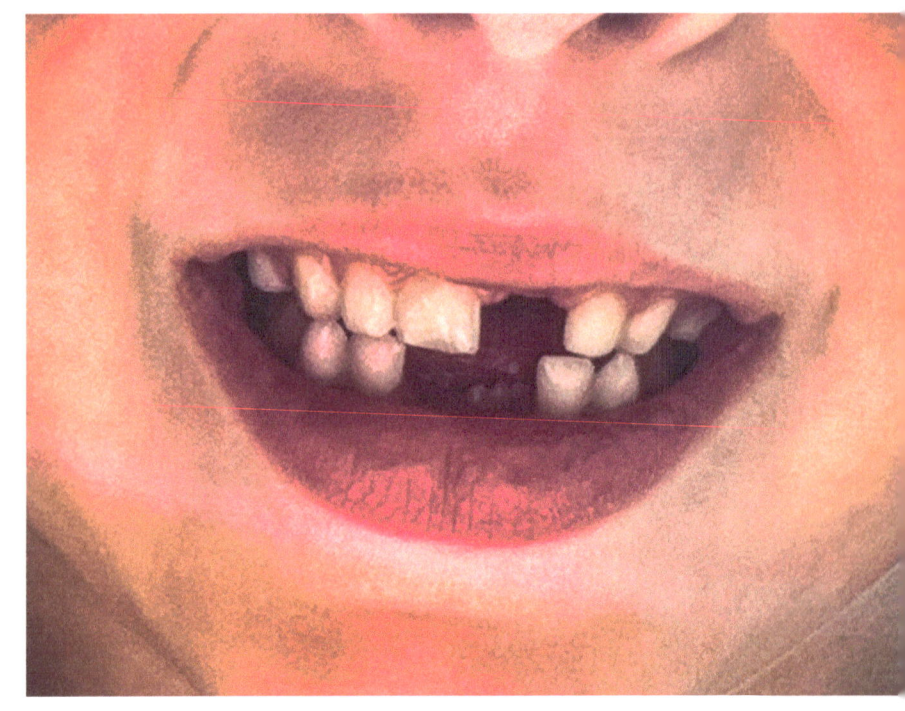

Adolescence & Aging

Room for growth.
Timeless.

Paint my spirits with your brilliance, your candor.
Tell me our flesh was once soft as velvet, fresh.
Lure me down the path
where today will blossom into another
so we may reminisce.

March of Time

Not everyone can boast of a polio portfolio.
Mine was established at the age of three.
Former president Franklin D. Roosevelt
had to wait until he was thirty-nine.

It's non-discriminating
from actors to artists, scientists to musicians.

There were periods of isolation, loneliness,
pain, and uncertainty, long before the coronavirus.

Note: In 1938, the March of Dimes, a campaign to eradicate poliomyelitis, was named by comedian Eddie Cantor after a radio show titled The March of Time. Hollywood backed the campaign in celebration of FDR's annual Birthday Ball, appealing to listeners of all incomes to send a dime or more to the cause. To date, the March of Dimes continues its commitment to prevent birth defects, helping over 75,000 families a year.

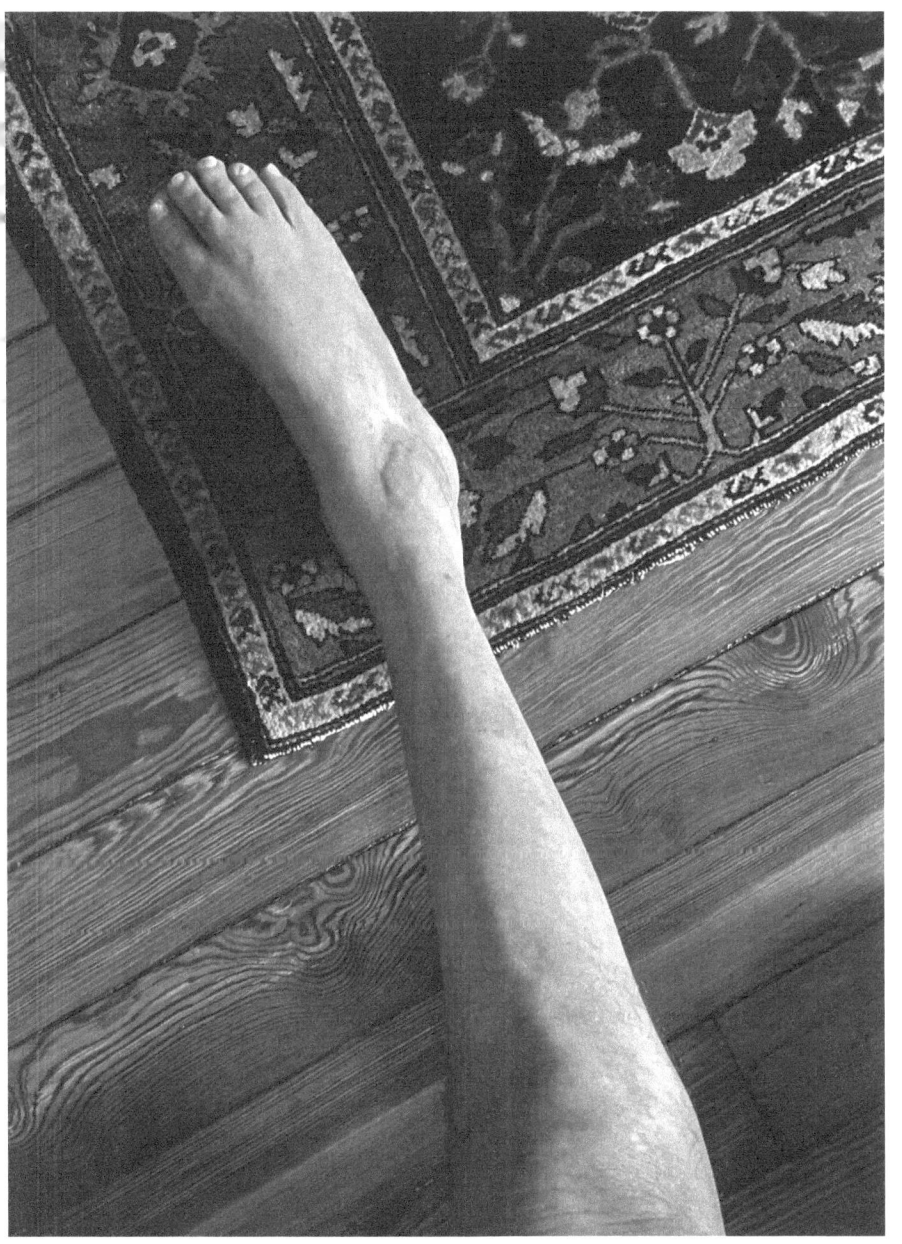

Living proof, the aged offer nourishment
and shelter for the young.
Something to cling to and to grow from.

Come, sit with me.
Though worn
I am ingrained to rock and coax
a story, a memory
into these arms of mine.

No one has ever performed a solo without first being in tune with those who will listen.

Waltzing Through Time

Three favorite artifacts
a shoehorn, a motorcycle, and a dinosaur.

Three after three, time reimagined
Three siblings, three children
A moment of reflection, of gratitude
for those who've come before, from, and after me.

The Heart of To-Matter

Living with purpose is essential to our heart
just as our heart is essential to living.
Plant thoughts and intentions for well-being.
Quantity over quality matters not.

Mother nature has proven the red pepper is
gender neutral and STEM certified!

Peaceable Possibility

Over and over again
Humanity
Sets the stage
To re-enact war
Instead of peace
Upon each other.

Bone Collector's Prayer

May all who once roamed free live in eternal peace.
To those who come across my bones,
know I am grateful to have seen the beauty in the world.
To have honored the living and the dead.
Amen

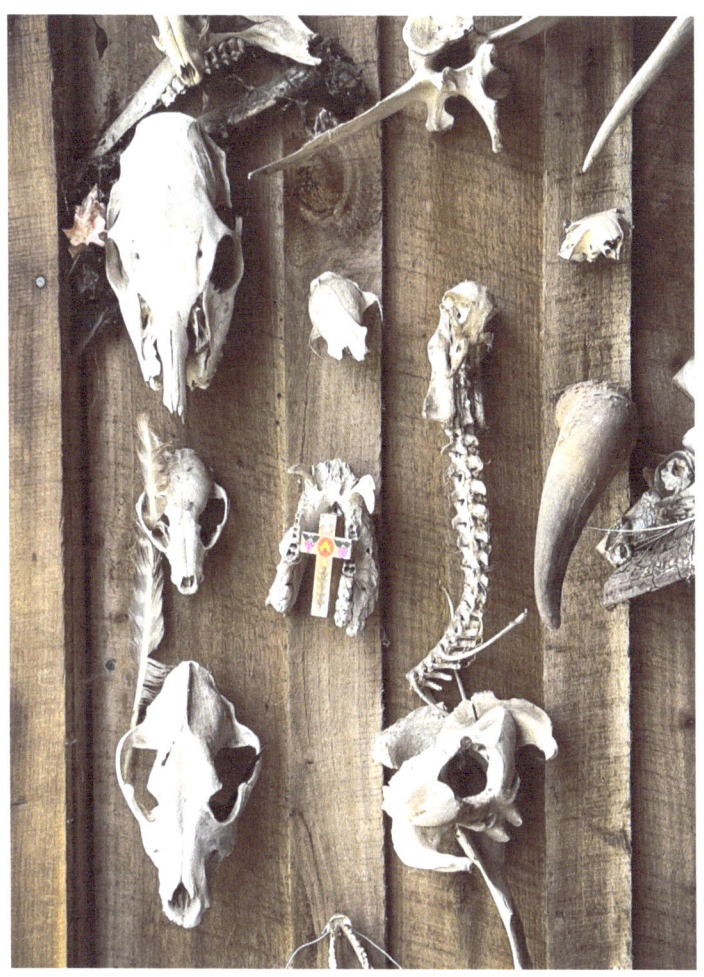

Emotional Void

A reminder, a record
countless lives are hard-driven.

Selection Process

Take thoughts and flowers.
When not perfect or beginning to whither
we discard them,
tell them to hit the road
so we may raise our vibration.

Temptation in moderation.
A medicinal confection
to sugarcoat your ailments.

Spinning

Hold on
but not too tight,
enough to know your roots,
enough to let you soar.

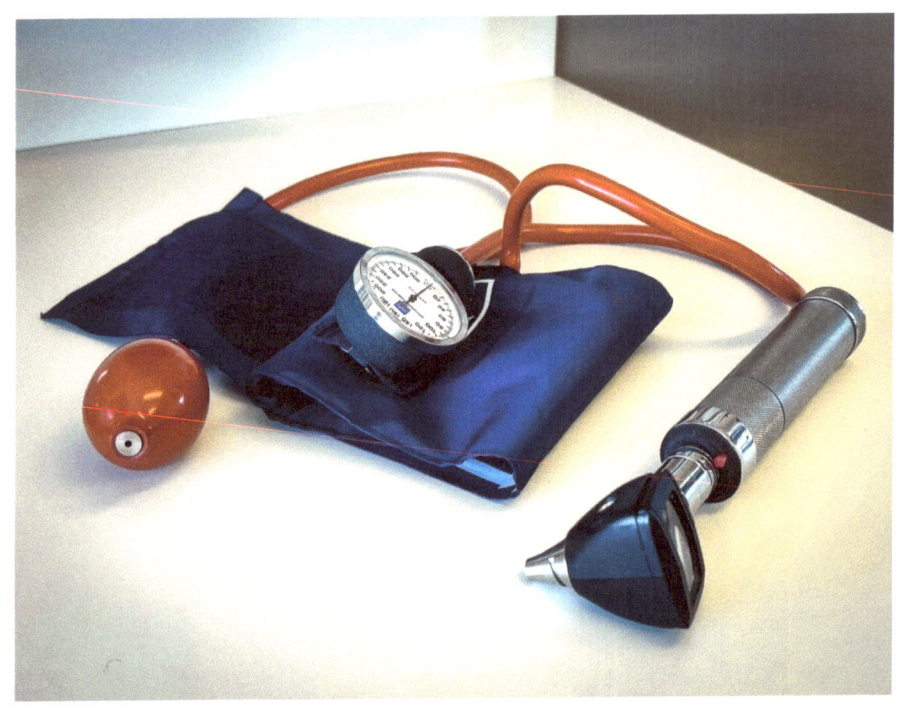

Red, White, and Blue

Freedom to maintain our body
Be it virtual or in-person
Immunized or not
There is pressure

Pipe Dreams

These pipes may not be your dream
but somewhere, someone's dream
is coming to fruition.
Soon they'll be buried
with the flow.
Nonexistent.

"I have always held respect and curiosity
for people older than I, feeling there's always
something to be learned from their experiences.
As you know, age brings wisdom. I grew up in
a household with a strong sense of equality.
My parents were both educators and great
examples of teamwork. My education emphasized
leadership and self-determination. To this day,
I love listening to those that have lived and
grown thru different worlds."

Terry Wild

January 28, 2022

Plant vs. Plant

Grown like weeds
Taking over
choking out the good, assumably for the better.

Sometimes it's easier to see things in black and white.

About the Photographer

Terry Wild of Lexington, Kentucky, is the owner of Terry Wild Stock, a picture agency specializing in image placements, fine print leasing, and limited-edition print sales. His career as a commercial photographer commenced in 1972 with the founding of The Wild Studio, specializing in commercial and editorial photography. He graduated from Lycoming College in Williamsport, Pennsylvania, and the Art Center College of Design in Pasadena, California. His work is known, collected, and published internationally.

"Photography has always been my second language. The natural and social landscape has been my theme, and form, texture, design, and composition, my vocabulary."

Terry's photography spans a variety of styles and disciplines, ranging from regional and national landscapes, flora, and nature studies to editorial landscapes and sociological commentary. He now works digitally, producing limited-edition archival pigment prints on acid-free fine art paper.

A photographic journey of over fifty years, Terry's work is a testament to documenting the changes in our natural and social landscapes while embracing changing technology. Terry exclusively used his iPhone to create project *Seventy-Five*.

For more information, go to https://www.terrywildstock.com/

About the Author

Pennsylvania native Lori Joseph studied visual communications and graphic design at the Art Institute of Pittsburgh. Joseph has lived in eight states, and her career as a photo stylist has taken her throughout the country where she's collected inspiration. She discovered her love for writing while living on the plains of Nebraska.

Released in May 2020, Joseph's first book, *My Embrace*, is a book of inspiring stories, thoughts, and poems about living with fear, compassion, humor, and love. Joseph's poetry has been published by the National League of American Pen Women, *Like Sunshine After Rain* anthology, *Pen in Hand* literary journal of the Maryland Writers' Assoc., the NWG anthology *Voices From the Plains*, 2nd edition, *How it Looks from Here: Poetry from the Plains*, the *Open Window Review*, *Clerestory Poetry Journal: Poems of the Mountain West*, and the Union Pacific Railroad.

Joseph collaborated with photographers Tim O'Hara and Terry Wild to create the Homestead Collection, a touring ekphrastic collection of work exhibited in Wyoming, Massachusetts, and Maryland.

In addition to poetry, she has created a collection of two-minute inspirational messages for podcasts and has aired on WMUG radio.

Visit Joseph's Amazon author page,
https://www.amazon.com/Lori-Joseph/e/B0881XN88B,
to learn more.

 J²B Publishing

ISBN: 978-1-954682-37-5

.

www.ingramcontent.com/pod-product-compliance
Lightning Source LLC
Chambersburg PA
CBHW041409010726
47507CB00001B/56

‍ * 9 7 8 1 9 5 4 6 8 2 3 7 5 *